FINANCIALLY
WORTHY

EDUCATING AND EMPOWERING WOMEN
TO BECOME THEIR OWN FINANCIAL AMBASSADORS

LAYNIE JOHNSON

No part of this publication may be reproduced, stored in a retrieval system, or transmitted in any form or by any means – electronic, photocopying, recording, or otherwise – without prior written permission, except in the case of brief excerpts in critical reviews and articles. For permission requests, contact the author at simplylaynie@gmail.com.

IG: Simplylaynie

ISBN: 9781689436304

The author disclaims responsibility for adverse effects or consequences from the misapplication or injudicious use of the information contained in this book. Mention of resources and associations does not imply an endorsement.

This book is dedicated to my daughter, Sophia.

I can't tell you to reach for your worth
without claiming my own.

My commitment is to model this to you
by my actions, not my words.

TABLE OF CONTENTS

INTRODUCTION

Have you ever felt financial freedom was an unattainable goal for you?

Have you ever felt that you were working hard and couldn't catch a break?

Have you ever dreamed of having financial independence?

Have you ever been scared of what making money would do to you?

Have you ever felt, deep down, that you might not be worthy of wealth?

These are some of the many questions that I have struggled with in my life. I cannot begin to explain where this notion of lack of worthiness seeped into my life, but it did. I grew up with big goals of what I wanted my life to be. My head was filled with the child-like fantasies that I presume most girls have. At some point, however, some limiting beliefs crept in, and I stopped believing I could live a bold and audacious life. Those limiting beliefs framed me and subconsciously impacted the choices I would make. My beliefs were deeply rooted in society's judgments and created an expectation of what my abilities could be based on my gender. In some deep place within me, I believed I was not supposed to dream big dreams or create a significant impact on the world.

Some things happened as I envisioned and some just eluded me. Although I had these wild dreams, I approached life with a more modest mindset. Failure was something that scared me. This fear prevented me from taking risks as I anchored more deeply into my deep-seated limiting beliefs. These beliefs stripped me of my wild dreams and created a safer haven in which I could live comfortably, but also below my potential. I am sure you have heard this, but nothing good ever comes from a comfort zone.

Working in financial services for over 15 years, I have seen this struggle with worthiness as a theme that is common with women. I have noticed that women who come into money tend to give it away, while other women seem to lose any money they make. In general, it seems that women struggle to accept money into their lives, and this is something I want to change. It's as if when money enters the equation for women, the scarcity mindset takes control.

My experience has shown that women view money as an intimidating subject. My clients who are more artistic (creative) are even more intimidated by the subject. The topic just goes over their head, or perhaps they were trained by society to think that it was too complicated. In general, though, women seem to have certain barriers with respect to money. These are a few of the barriers I have seen consistently in my female clients:

Barrier 1: Lack of Confidence

Women radiate competence and authority on the career front by gaining market share in so many sectors, but when it comes to money, not so much. I have asked so many successful women about their perception of money. They all say the same thing: it is overcomplicated, and the vernacular that is used in financial services intimidates them. The notion of investing in the stock market is overwhelming, and after seeing so many stories of public figures who have tainted the industry as a whole, they question whether they can really trust financial advisors.

"Where do I even begin?"

"How much do I need to hit a monumental goal?"

"How much do I need to save to retire when I want to?"

"I don't feel like I could ever do it."

I have also seen women who are afraid to ask the questions. Have you ever been in an appointment with your doctor who rattles off a medical term and you are completely lost? You ask for another explanation and the terminology is over your head. You simply cannot digest what you have just been told. Why is this? Because it's personal. It could be life changing for you. The same is true with money. It's personal and critical to your livelihood. It can be the component that changes your life. It enables you to live the way you want. It facilitates how you and your family reach goals and necessities. However, it can't be used for those purposes unless you understand what it is and how to make it work for you.

The lack of confidence is also a result of society stereotypes. Even some of the most capable women can become self-doubters when we talk about our money. This is an understandable reaction to the relative inaccessibility of the male-dominated financial world. Most women that I know, or have worked with, look at the prospectus that comes with the investments and immediately get lost. The abstract language and terms overwhelm them and causes them to shut down or flee. This lack of knowledge further decreases their confidence.

I have also found that so many women feel intimidated, and that intimidation causes them to be paralyzed. If they can even come up with any questions, they become afraid to ask them because they don't want to sound dumb. In addition, I have had countless clients tell me that in meetings with other financial advisors, the professional speaks mainly to the husband. Equally bothersome are financial professionals speaking over the clients with terminology that might as well be Greek.

If money-related discussions make you feel nervous or uncomfortable, I encourage you to talk about money more, not less. I have found one of the only ways to eliminate intimidation surrounding the subject matter is to lean into it more. Talk about money regularly with your spouse, family member, or close friend, and also find resources to educate yourself on the subject.

I also highly encourage having a trusted advisor that you can lean on. A financial professional who is versed in the subject matter, current economic trends, and current tax implications will greatly maximize your success for the future. Focus on working with someone who strips the jargon and makes it clear and easy to understand. You want someone you feel 100% comfortable working with.

The biggest confidence builder with money is knowledge. *Knowledge is power.* Start small by simply looking at your financial statements. Look at the inserts that financial service companies place in your statements. Often, sound bites will be added based on the time of year. During the tax season months, the inserts might include helpful tips for tax season. Consider looking up a few financial professionals and watch content from these people. You might also read up on specific topics. We are living in the best time for gathering knowledge because so many resources are available to us.

Barrier 2: Don't Overthink it!

The notion of being smart with money for women has traditionally meant maximizing each dollar. The idea that men earn the money and women decided how to spend it still exists today. Not much has changed in this area. Women still make most of the household purchases and are geniuses in finding bargains. Sales and savings provide a euphoric gratification for women. To me, it circles back to the saving component. A short-term deal is worth far less than a smart investment for your future. I am a huge advocate of making good use of money. I also have a huge passion for helping women think bigger and stop worrying about the small stuff. Similar to any other area of our lives, we grow as we continue to lean into hard areas. What we do repeatedly enhances our ability to learn and amend past mistakes.

Barrier 3: Waiting for someone else to come to the rescue

This one hits home for me, and I am a living testimony to this. I find a lot of women are raised to believe that their husbands will handle the finances. A small percentage of the population was raised by mothers who were the sole financial decision makers. I also find most parents did not counsel their daughters about saving or investing. Society just seems to believe that men will be responsible for investing, long-term savings, and home purchases. I even find that some married women ignore issues around money until they are forced to pay attention. Sadly, this moment of necessity often comes when you are the least emotionally prepared to deal with it, such as when you have lost a spouse or are going through a divorce. Unfortunately, for many women, it takes a life-altering event to ignite a change in behavior.

According to a Prudential Research Study, fewer than two in 10 women feel "very prepared" to make wise financial decisions. Half indicate that they "need some help," and one-third feel that they "need a lot of help." (*http://www. smartmoneychicks.com/1281/statistics-women-and-money/*)

This is what fuels me. This is what has me so passionate about equipping women to step into their best financial self. I can also tell you that every risk I took financially did not mean I was 100% ready. But guess what? I always figured it out. I will say you have to have some discipline around this. Keeping slightly ahead of what is comfortable but not hugely out of range is key. I emphasize this because I understand that if we waited until we were truly ready, nothing would happen. A little bit of angst and fear can be the best motivators. Every time I pushed myself out of my comfort zone, it became my incentive to work a little harder, and I felt great satisfaction in what I accomplished. I want you to have this same sense of pride. I once heard a speaker say, "I am here to comfort the uncomfortable and disturb the comfortable." I have noticed that women shrink away from uncomfortable or intimidating topics. Too often I have seen women in duress because of a triggering event (death or divorce) and suddenly need the most sound advice on one of the most important subjects – money. Yet it happens when they are in their most vulnerable state. I want women to be empowered before this happens. The time to be armored up is before you begin the war.

Barrier 4: Focused on Goals, not Numbers

The layout of financial statements usually focuses on bold numbers in certain categories such as Account Totals or Performance. Women want to make money just as much as any man, but we also want to know how to track our goals. Our focus is not so much the number on the statement but the tangible goal we are trying to reach. In addition, there seems to be a 'safety' valve woven into the female DNA which leads us to search for security and certainty in order to calm our worries.

"Can I afford the car or house?"

"Can I afford the vacation?"

"Do I have enough money to send my children to college?"

"Am I on target for retirement?"

"Will I run out of money?"

These are some of the concrete goals that seem most important to women. The financial conversations about saving and investing that we have with our financial professional or spouse needs to be directly connected to the results we want to see in our lives. This is why I am a huge advocate for encouraging women to think specifically about what you would do with a sudden infusion of wealth. Make financial goals as detailed as possible, including an estimated cost for each specific goal. Studies show this increases the likelihood of success and keeps you accountable. It is the same concept as manifesting. To me, being financially savvy doesn't have to be about making more money just to increase my bottom line. I redirect my clients to think about money as a tool to get you closer to achieving goals, taking care of yourself and the people you love.

Many people have told me through the years that I should write a book about my experience. It seemed crazy to me the first time I heard it – like *bananas* crazy! But today, it seems more important than ever to share what I have learned. Women need to understand their worthiness and develop confidence to improve their lives and their financial bottom line. If this sounds like you, then keep reading. My hope is that in the following pages you will find ideas and tips that make sense to you, ideas that you can begin to implement right now in your life.

If you follow my guidelines and listen to my advice, I believe you will come to know and believe in yourself, and ultimately, discover your financial worth so that you can anchor into this truth.

Barrier 5: Wealth Accumulation isn't for Women

Over my years working in Investment Management, I have witnessed all the subliminal messages that seem to make women think being wealthy isn't achievable for them. Despite the gender money gaps, I have witnessed societal norms that suggest wealth isn't for women. This barrier is the one I would most like to eliminate. I have encountered countless women who tell me they are ready to build wealth but feel the cards are stacked against them. Although I feel a lot of this has to do with mindset, I cannot help but see the way in which society has contributed to this. The most vivid example that I have is when the Teen Talk Barbie edition was released in 1992. The Barbie said a few statements including, "Math class is tough." I remember this distinctly because of the controversy that ensued after the doll was released. Women are gaining more and more market share in almost every area. So my question is, why not in your own balance sheet?

Your story does not have to stop with any of these limiting beliefs. I sincerely hope this book can be one of many resources that help you overcome those beliefs and build your wealth!

FIND YOUR WORTH

Chapter 1

Ditch the Victim Mentality

Looking back on my life, I recognize that I used to work so hard at garnering approval from others while also trying to be all things to all people. What I was left with was a shell of what I was really designed to be. They say you cannot pour from an empty cup, yet somehow, some way, I figured out how to continue to give while being completely depleted myself. Of course, it came with a cost. Deep down I knew this was not sustainable, yet I did not understand the "why" behind my behavior. According to Webster's Dictionary, the definition of people pleaser is "a person who has an emotional need to please others often at the expense of his or her own needs or desires." (https://www.merri-am-webster.com/dictionary/people%20pleaser) After years of working on myself through therapy and self-discovery, I realized people pleasing and lack of worth were directly correlated. I yearned for a way to solve this problem in my life, but I wasn't able to clearly articulate it.

My upbringing certainly contributed to this behavior. I cannot necessarily pinpoint the exact origin, but at some point in my life, I learned that I had to be perfect. I grew up in a home filled with love as well as challenges. I am mindful of how I want to share some of these details, as this is not just my story. I will say that parts of my childhood were difficult and painful. To some extent, my parents were emotionally unavailable to me growing up. I believe this is when I subconsciously began to form the people pleasing trait. I never questioned if I was loved. I knew that. But like many of us, my family had dysfunction and dynamics that deeply impacted me.

I am the youngest of three girls. I was the bold one of the three. My sisters would dare me to jump into the pool when it was windy and cold, and I did it. My sisters encouraged me to ask some famous person at a Dodgers game for his autograph. I didn't even know who this old man was, but I did it. I was not easily intimidated, and that, along with my boldness, were strong traits that became somewhat muted over time.

My two older sisters set the bar high. As the youngest, I looked up to them with deep admiration. Their success seemed effortless to me. We all went to the same elementary school and every summer I would pray that my teachers would be different than those who taught my sisters. I felt labeled as a "Johnson girl," which instantly made every part of my body cringe knowing the expectation that came with that label. I was the student in school who had to work really hard. I did well, but it was more my hustle and perseverance that won out. I was not naturally gifted when it came to school. I worked diligently and hard to excel, but I also felt that I was shadowed in the expectation of being as good as my older sisters. I felt I never measured up. I felt as if I was not enough. I elected to go to an entirely different high school because I wanted desperately to find my own identity. I wanted to be in an environment where no one knew my sisters. I wanted to feel I was not marked with any labels. Perhaps we have all felt this way at some point in life.

My father had high expectations of me, and I never wanted to let him down. As a young girl, his approval was all I wanted. My dad could look at me and say 1000 words without one of them leaving his lips. I never wanted that look. The feeling of disappointing him left a pit in my stomach.

Still, as I was growing up, I had these larger than life ideas of how my life would turn out. My visions included becoming a CEO of a company, creating massive impact on the world, and having a picture-perfect life. As a very young girl, I planned my wedding a thousand times in my head. I even had the white picket house selected, and my future family was all carefully planned out. If you had asked me at age five what I thought I would be when I grew up, I would have answered, without hesitation, that I was going to be the president of the United States.

But somewhere between the ages of seven and 17, I absorbed all the beliefs and lies that stripped me of being who I could be. During those years, I knew that I was not living the life I was capable of, but instead, I settled for how things were. Rather than push through the fear and go for the gusto, I rooted in this fear. The gravity of that feeling shackled me deeper and deeper into this lie. I spent my life resenting others who had more than I did or had the seemingly perfect life. I was filled with toxic thoughts that did not serve me. I was a victim of my own making.

Without realizing it, I found ways to reinforce these notions. I allowed others' beliefs and societal stereotypes to seep into my being. That "balls to the wall" girl of my younger years was somehow silenced inside of me, and I lost that audacious confidence and my sense of worth. I didn't even realize that I was creating limiting beliefs that reconfigured the trajectory of my life. It was not until years later that I learned that the subconscious mind does not know the difference between a truth and a lie.

What I have learned over the years is that when we root ourselves in a victim mentality without clear resolve, we relinquish all our power. Anytime we are in a victim mentality, we lose productivity to sitting in that mindset and wallowing in it. It means we are focused on the wrong things, and as a result, we produce nothing useful. Of course, in my case, I usually get pretty defensive and blaming when I am in this mentality as well. Have you ever heard some self-help guru say that life is either happening *to* you or *for* you? When you understand that life is working for you, it makes you realize that victim mindset is a total lie. Remember: it is never too late to forge a new path. We always hold the power to implement a shift, to redirect, and even to start over. There is no shame in having gone the wrong way, but there is hope in creating new outcomes.

Eventually I entered the career force, and in my naiveté, was surprised to encounter people who did not embody the same work ethic that I had. It was astonishing to me. This is when I learned the harsh reality that not everyone has the same commitment to excellence. Nonetheless, I continued on my path but stumbled into conflicts as I was learning how to work with people on an entirely new playing field. The limiting beliefs that weighed my self-worth down were only reinforced as such conflicts erupted in my life.

I wrestled with this lack of self-esteem and worth in so many areas of my life. It prevented me from acting, taking risks, and living my life without fear. I was so afraid to fail that I did nothing for the longest time. I was in a state of constant struggle. The whimsical and dreamy part of my personality imagined this wildly successful life, yet my inner dialogue kept me shackled to this notion that I was not enough. The lie that I was not enough became louder and more detrimental for me.

It was not until I started to take massive action that the narrative began to change in my head. Once I changed that narrative, all things began to work in greater force to build my self-worth. I watched a documentary about a well-known boxer, and he talked about his inner circle. He said he only surrounded himself with people who believed he could win. That message stayed with me, and I slowly took inventory of how people were impacting my life. I focused on the five major people in my circle and paid close attention to who I was allowing into that circle.

Focusing on my own personal development, I began to study self-help professionals and root deeper in my faith. I had strayed from my faith as I thought God was leaving me high and dry. What I did not realize is the gifts I embodied were God-given. That unrelenting ambition that I have was not of my own making. I also learned that no matter what your circumstances were growing up, you are still in control of your life. These self-help "gurus" taught me that the "junk" that I had allowed to block me was under my control. I could choose to leave my path blocked or I could make the decision to remove the "junk." This realization was a breakthrough in stepping into my own worth. Once I truly ditched that victim mentality, I began to find opportunity and reclaim my power. Discovering the power allowed me to break through periods of transition with strength and a stronger sense of my own worth.

Once I began to accept this concept, I also began to make money. At first, it was an uncomfortable feeling for me. I was so conditioned to living paycheck to paycheck that I didn't know what to do. Without knowing it then, I can now see that I had a scarcity mindset. The truth was that my innermost being was still battling with the idea that I was not worthy of this success. Finally being in a place where I was making money was a foreign concept to me. I began giving money away as if I was a billionaire. Even though I am a giving person and believe in paying it forward, I was doing it with the wrong motives. Instead of giving from a place of abundance, I was doing it out of fear and scarcity. I was also doing it to get people to like me. It sounds silly, but it is the truth. It wasn't long before I realized that I needed to stop this self-sabotaging behavior and really work on being my own financial ambassador and steward of my money.

Have you ever been encouraged to push out of your comfort zone? And even with a glimpse of excitement, you are still incredibly nervous? Have you ever felt in your deepest core that the very thing that scares you will yield the most growth? This is how I felt, and it was that feeling which led to the most pivotal moment of my career.

CHAPTER 2

FIND YOUR VOICE

I began working jobs not for the sake of finding a career or purpose, but mainly so I did not have to move home with my parents. I enjoyed living away from my parents, as most kids who leave the nest do. I always felt my parents had high expectations of me, and I did not want to disappoint. As you will see throughout my story, the people pleaser in me is always present. I worked a job for a company that was a subsidiary of Nike. It was a really fun job and a great environment. Then my position was eliminated and, as a result, I learned a new term – severance pay. This was a rather cool concept to me. I received a lump sum of money as a part of my layoff package. I also foolishly cashed out my 401k as I had no financial acumen. I paid hefty taxes and it was a costly mistake that could have been avoided if I had the knowledge I have now. Honestly, I am not sure that I would have made the right choice even if I had been equipped with the knowledge because I also had this youth complex. I believed that I was young, and I could outlive any bad choices. It is very easy to look back now and think, "If only I did not feel the money topic was taboo. If only I had the courage to ask questions versus feeling ill-equipped. If only I had known what I know now, then that money could have compounded." Again, having no real discipline with money, I felt like I won the lottery, and I lived like that, too.

Soon I was running out of money and time, and I was getting rather anxious. I did not want to have to tell my parents of my poor choices or dare ask for help. I began asking my friends if the companies they worked for were hiring. This was before the internet, so placement agencies and word-of-mouth were the best routes to find jobs. I had a friend who worked for an investment bank and provided a contact for me to inquire about employment. This is what I like to refer to as "how my career path began."

It was not until years later that I realized I accidentally fell into my passion. I worked in several capacities before becoming an assistant for a financial advisor at that big investment bank. I was eager to learn all I could, as my desire to serve his client base was high. As a people pleaser at heart, I had a deep need for validation. Born with a really strong work ethic, I wanted to please my boss and do exceptional work for his clients. I quickly became eager to learn more about investment management, but really did not have a deep understanding of money at all.

Growing up, money was not a topic that was openly discussed. It actually felt like it was taboo. As a result of this, I learned to place my head in the sand when it came to money. I was raised to be respectful of people's financial means. I was taught not to ask invasive questions. I was also the kid who received birthday money and spent it before it touched my hands. I lived with an instant gratification mindset, and I had no concept of money. I did not really think past my current desire. My dad once made me work to buy designer clothing that all the kids had, but even that exercise was fleeting as I moved on to the next thing I wanted.

I was vulnerable prey when I entered college and credit card companies were offering credit. I can still vividly remember walking down campus to the student center. The walkway was lined with tables, balloons, and giveaways to lure you into applying for credit. I felt like a kid in a candy store. Of course, I walked closer and found myself with a clipboard completing an application. "Buy now and pay later" sounded great to me. Sign me up all day long and twice on Sunday. Inevitably, I fell victim to that downward cycle. I racked up about $4,000 in credit card debt over my time in college. I could barely scrape together enough money to pay the minimum amount every month. I took cash advances on those cards not realizing the hefty APR fees accessed. After beginning a new role at the investment bank, I wanted this to change my financial blueprint. I wanted to improve my own financial habits and also to feel equipped to assist high net worth clients.

I worked in a few roles before an opening to work for one of the top advisors at the investment firm became available. I was encouraged by a few colleagues to apply for an internal job opening. It was intimidating, yet I knew I desired more of a challenging job.

During my interview process, I promised my advisor that I would take my Series 7 (known formally as the General Securities Representative Qualification Examination administered by FINRA, the Financial Industry Regulatory Authority) within a few months of acquiring this new position. Have you ever made a promise to fulfill something, and said the right thing in order to have a certain outcome? During the interview process for the job, I said what I knew he wanted to hear. I wanted it to be true, but at the same time, I was paralyzed with fear of failure and the unknown. I had watched several people fail this exam, and some were terminated as a result. I really wanted the job as his assistant but dreaded the idea of taking the tests.

Fortunately, I was given the position and bought the books to begin studying for the exam. However, they sat in the same place in my apartment, untouched. A few weeks into my new role, my boss came out of his office and kneeled at my desk. My heart raced as I knew what he was going to ask me. I was somehow hoping I could avoid this conversation. He asked me my timeline for taking the exam. Honestly, I was hoping to slowly slide into this role and get so busy training that taking the exam fell by the wayside. The people pleaser in me rattled off a date in a few weeks. It was like a knee jerk reaction. The truth was that I was terrified beyond measure to study or take this exam. I was afraid of failing and what people would think – my boss, mainly. I wrestled with the notion that I would be letting him down.

Looking back, I am so grateful for my dedication to my word, as that promise to my boss is what pushed me to act. I actually learned through this process that sometimes our weaknesses are also our strengths. The people pleaser in me, and my pride, allowed me to honor my word even though my head did not think I could. To combat the fear, I simply stepped into massive action. It was hard. I worked an eight-hour shift, studied for three to four hours every night, and did it all again the next day. I spent all of my weekends studying. I took a one-week crash course. Following the instructor's recommendation, I scheduled my exam a week after completing the course and followed the road map for the exam preparation the instructor laid out. On the practice final that I took before my exam, I was right on the cusp of a passing score. Of course, I was panicked and scared. I called the instructor, and he encouraged me to take the exam as scheduled. He said he believed in me. I remember hanging up the phone feeling like I was borrowing his belief.

Of course, I told no one that my exam was scheduled as I was worried I would not pass. I even scheduled my exam for a Saturday so I would not need to ask for a day off. This also helped me be stealthy about taking the exam. I was so tempted to cancel, and I even called the exam center four times before hanging up. I knew deep down that if I rescheduled the exam, I would never take the test. I would continue to find a reason to push back the date. In the end, I kept the scheduled date and continued to study.

The night before the exam, I watched the movie "Wall Street," as I wanted no other material entering my mind. Of course, I didn't sleep well that night. The next morning, I walked into the exam center, shaking. A man signed in at the same time. He was older and made a flippant remark about me not being able to pass the exam. (I only insert that here as a sidebar. We will always have people pulling at us to keep us from achieving our goals. Press on!)

For some remarkable miracle, his words did not penetrate me that morning. I was laser focused. As the exam began, it took me a few minutes to calm myself, but then I began to get into the zone. When it was time to take the thirty-minute mandatory break, I didn't want to go. I just wanted to finish. Going back in after the break, I kept going until I was done. As I came to the last screen, I paused a moment before hitting the "submit" button. This was it. I had done all I could, and now it was time to see what would happen. I took one last deep breath and pressed the button. The screen went blank. My heart skipped a beat, and I felt the panic start to rise up inside me. For 10 seconds, the blank screen stared back at me, and I felt like I couldn't breathe. Then suddenly, in small 10-point font on the upper right side of the screen, the word popped up – Passed!

I was elated, and I wanted to jump up and down right there! The relief was inexplicable. So many mixed emotions flooded into my body, and I wanted to cry and scream. As I was checking out, the girl at the testing center whispered to me that the guy who gave me grief did not pass. I have too often allowed others' comments to impact me adversely when that was a choice I made. This was another example that reminded me external comments do not hold weight over my life unless I allow it. Maybe it will also serve as a reminder for you to press on and ignore all that does not serve you.

Leaving the exam center, I slowly got into my car. The door was barely shut before the tears began to well up and spill down my cheeks. All the feelings I had been holding in over the past few weeks flooded over me, and in the fiber of my being, I knew my life was going to change from taking *and passing* that exam.

To place a little more context on this time of my life, I had overcome some major low points in my life. I had battled with feeling sorry for myself that I had not yet found "Mr. Right." It seemed that all of my friends were getting married, and I felt anchored to being the single friend. It felt like life was eluding me. The downward spiral of my mindset had me focusing on "this isn't fair." My sister encouraged me to keep pressing on. She would often say to me, "Around the bend, life will be different." It was a phrase I held close to my heart after passing the exam.

Walking to my car that day, I felt that phrase actually come to life for me. I had a new sense of hope and excitement. I felt like that little girl who believed she could accomplish anything. I felt this sense of hope that I cannot begin to describe. The seeds of worthiness were being replanted. Wiping away my tears, I realized I couldn't wait to call my family and friends to tell them that I had passed. I also called the advisor I worked for to tell him. He, of course, was very happy for me. I had so much energy that I went to the gym and worked it off on the treadmill.

Passing this exam did wonders for my self-esteem and confidence. I began to study and attain the other licenses that I needed to advance in the industry. I did not take a break. I wanted the momentum of that invincible feeling to carry over for the next wave of exams. What began as a job for me was turning into a career without me really knowing it.

After obtaining my licenses, the trajectory of my career did change. I began to voraciously learn about all aspects of the financial markets. I was fascinated with the planning tools to create investment portfolios that were in alignment with a client's goals. I felt like an artist with a blank canvas, and I had the opportunity and ability to turn what they had into a masterpiece.

Time continued to progress, and I became more and more interested in my advisor's practice. I quickly figured out that the more the advisor made, the more I could potentially earn. I began to focus on streamlining his practice. The advisor noticed my efforts and offered me a role as junior partner. I was elated, and that confidence allowed me to continue to grow and uncover the business opportunities within his practice. As I began to get more involved with clients, my passion for what I was doing grew as well. I learned more and more. The result of this was that I was slowly coming to a place where the dynamic with my work partner was shifting. I became less concerned with what he thought of me. I found a passion in being the facilitator to constructing comprehensive wealth management solutions for families. I had a new focus and purpose in helping others, and it changed everything.

During this time, I also noticed that my pay had actually declined as a junior partner versus what I had made as a portfolio associate. This is the moment that got my attention. I began to seek counsel from other advisors and mentors. One of my mentors gave me some very strong advice to work on improving my equity within my partnership. I spent the next several months trying to negotiate a fair split with my partner and a clear business plan for growth. These were some of the most grueling months for me, but I learned so much from the experience. Ultimately, my partner and I were not able to come to an agreement on a fair split of the partnership, and it was in that moment that I knew I needed to change my direction.

I am condensing a very hard season of my life into a sound bite as I describe this time period. I tried everything to come up with a fair solution with my partner. I consulted with experts in my industry and had a mentor who gave me sound advice. With every plea and attempt with my partner, I was shot down in a rather degrading manner. I remember the moment that my mentor said to me, "You need to go out on your own." I froze. I was almost mad. He sat silently while I processed what he had just said. He then looked at me and recapped all the solutions that I had proposed without any traction from my partner. I was driving solid growth in the partnership. My mentor said to me, "Why are you allowing yourself to be so undervalued?" At that point my mentor asked if I had a "Plan B." I paused, trying to understand why he asked that. Then it hit me: I was giving away my work, which meant I was essentially giving away my worth.

My mentor has become a dear friend, and we joke about this now, but at the time, I was only just coming to the realization that I had outgrown the relationship. Deep down, I knew I was made for more and that I had endless possibilities ahead of me. It was just starting to dawn on me that this partnership was no longer serving my future or me.

It was scary to think of leaving that partnership and trying to build a client base at a new firm, but I began looking for other opportunities while maintaining a game face with my work partner. The relevancy here is that in order to discover my worth, I needed to remove any internal or external factors that were trying to strip me of it. I knew I was stepping into my own, and I felt the excitement of the opportunity ahead. When the time was right, I made my move and will describe it in more detail in the chapters ahead. The lesson I learned in the process, however, is that self-worth is directly correlated with net worth. Struggling with worthiness for most of my life, I never realized this lack of worthiness directly impacted my ability to earn and sustain money. I used to believe that having a good work ethic would eventually yield higher compensation. Although in theory this sounds good, I have learned over my career that you have to ask for your worth.

I began to shop the market to see what was available to me, speaking to recruiters and contacting all the big investment firms. After months of my own due diligence, I selected the big investment bank that I planned to join. According to strict financial industry regulations, you are not allowed to tell clients or even suggest that you will be moving. You are held to a protocol standard for what information you can legally take. Essentially the day you select to resign, you give your notice and you are done. My decision to leave was a big risk, and I was nervous, but I could not stay where I was any longer. The fear of staying became greater than the fear of leaving. This is how I knew it was time.

On the day I gave notice, I was nervous. I had rehearsed what I was going to say over and over in my mind for months leading up to this moment. Due to industry standards, I was to give my resignation to the branch manager of our office. My manager was typically in before the opening of the stock market at about 6:30 a.m., but unfortunately, not on this day. Having to wait escalated my nerves even more. Finally, the branch manager walked by my office, and I felt so much relief. As I walked into his office, my hands were shaking so badly that I could hardly hold the file that contained my resignation letter and all the protocol documents. Still, I walked forward and did what I had to do. I paused for a moment, told my manager I was resigning, and then dropped the file on his desk. I elected not to have any interaction with my partner on that day. I had spent so much time agonizing over this decision, and I was afraid if I spoke to him, he would try and convince me to stay. The relationship between us had hit such a point of contention that I was confident I was making the best decision. As I turned and walked out, I held my head up high and maintained my composure. It was surreal to walk by people I had seen every day for the past several years, knowing this would be the last time I would likely see them.

Filled with uncertainty about whether I could actually build a business on my own, I was also determined to give it everything I had. I drove directly to my new office at my new firm and began calling clients, as I knew my former partner would be calling the clients to keep them as well. It would take a while for the clients to make their decisions, and during that time I built out my business plan and got acclimated with the new firm's technology. Over the next few weeks, I began to get more client engagement and was surprised to hear clients' comments about my former partnership. I also heard what my former partner was saying about me to clients. He attacked my investment acumen, my experience, my time in the industry, and my favorite slight, my gender. At first, it made me really angry and hurt my feelings. Fortunately, I had a mentor who set me straight. He told me to be grateful that my former advisor's words and actions were playing right into my hands. He was actually doing me a favor. Crazy, right? It was the truth. I allowed myself to stand in that truth and chose not to engage in that negativity. I began to receive support from other professionals, and within a few weeks, I began to receive notifications that clients were moving their assets to me. I was so grateful and full of excitement, and as a result, my confidence increased. I had control of my destiny, and I had discovered my passion. Engaging with a client and curating a comprehensive wealth management strategy for them is exactly what I was meant to do. I had a fire in my belly that was divinely placed, and I was following it. I anchored deeply in my faith and began to shift my focus from myself to how I could be of service to others.

Within the first six weeks of leaving my partnership, my business began to take off. During this time, I adopted a few intentional disciplines that made a huge difference for me. These practices are still a part of my daily routines. In the morning, after my devotional time and quiet meditation, I read 10 pages from a book focusing on development. My mentor also told me to write, "From this day forward I will solicit any client that needs my unique approach to wealth management," and to place this in multiple areas where I could see it daily. This was mainly to strip my psyche of the guilt I had for leaving my partner. I felt badly, even though I had given him ample opportunity to be fair. This guilt compounded the lack of worthiness that I had at that juncture of my story. I wrote it down on several pieces of paper and put them on my bathroom mirror, in my car, at my office, on my phone lock screen, and on my laptop. I literally retrained my brain, and my confidence increased even more. I was stepping into my own and finding my own voice. The biggest shift I learned in this period was to ditch the feeling of guilt and be unapologetic for my passion to be the private CFO to my clients.

CHAPTER 3

WRITE A NEW STORY

As I am writing this book, it has been almost six years since I made that shift. In hindsight, I can see that the partnership that had such a negative impact on my self-worth is also what gave me the courage to make a change. As my self-worth improved, so did my financial worth. In the first six months of being on my own, my income increased dramatically from what I had previously made. It blew my mind, and I was overwhelmed and incredibly grateful.

Of course, I was also in a new space, and it was scary to me. I know that sounds crazy to say it was scary to make money, but hear me out. It was foreign to me. I was terrified it would vaporize. In the ensuing months I had many mishaps with money. I found myself being frivolous in my spending. I succumbed to instant gratification. At one point I remember debating between two things I wanted, the Louis Vuitton Neverfull tote bag and the Cartier love bracelet. There was an internal battle going on which felt like the "good angel" on one shoulder versus the "tempting devil" on the other. I am grateful for the internal gauge in my framework as I could not bring myself to buy the bag or the bracelet. It wasn't that I was cheap, but rather that I recognized the power that came with being selective. I could simply never justify the expense. That selection process also helped me discover one of my anchoring truths about money.

If the item costs more than your mortgage and is not for your home as an upgrade or an expense for travel, then it doesn't happen.

As I questioned what I really wanted, I realized that I was feeding myself a false narrative that these "things" would actually make me "be someone." Once I realized that truth, they lost their appeal, and I began to create a new dialogue with money. I began to make a list of short-term and long-term desires, which in turn began the budgeting process in my life. Budgeting is a very personal practice, as what is important to one person can be vastly different from what is important to someone else. You will learn more about the practice of budgeting in Chapter 9, but for now, I just want you to recognize the importance of the process.

In the beginning, I wrote down every whimsical to practical desire. I then tracked every cent of my spending for a month. It was really an eye-opening experience for me. What I realized is how easy it is to spend without thinking in our culture. Big companies are constantly marketing to us and social media compounds that effect. How many times have you scrolled through Instagram and been tempted to shop for something you don't even need? Crazy, right? *Then the item that caught your eye appears in your feed as if your device is tempting you and spying on you.*

This is why this practice changed my life. After a month of tracking my expenses, I was shocked to see how I was wastefully spending money. I spent over $100 at Starbucks without even blinking. I justified this because I only ordered the iced coffee drink, which was far less than a specialty drink. It was shocking to realize I was spending close to $1200 a year on Starbucks!

It was during this time that an interview with Warren Buffett captured my interest. As a billionaire who lives a modest lifestyle, he intrigued me. In this interview, he talked about some of his habits and the creation of his wealth. He said he focused on having multiple income streams. Since he has been noted for his personal frugality despite his immense wealth, this discipline made sense to me and ultimately led to my dual-fold approach to finances.

By now you can see that my passion to teach and empower women to become their own financial ambassadors was birthed from my own experience. What I know is that aside from family, money is the next most important relationship you will ever have. When you view money as a relationship, it allows you to see it through another lens. Money is a facilitator. It is a means you can use to achieve different results. It enables you to live a certain way, to raise your family, to enjoy life, and so on. Understanding this concept is important if you want to shift your mindset about money.

Making financial decisions is intimidating, and if you're a woman who needs help with this process, then you are in the right place. In the next section, you are going to discover some ways you can change your relationship with money, overcome the fears you have, and learn the basic steps you need to take in order to build your finances.

CHAPTER 4

DISCOVER YOUR OWN SELF-WORTH

During the process of writing this book, I hit writer's block, came up against my lack of faith, and endured cycles of emotions, doubt, and fear. That little voice inside of me said, "Who do you think you are to write a book?" I had to mute my consumption of social media to stay in the zone. When I was really stuck, I reached out to my mentor and asked for help. As a good mentor does, he speaks in riddles. I often joke that he is like Mr. Miyagi from the movie *The Karate Kid*.

When I told him where I was stuck, he said, "At what age did you realize you were an overachiever?"

Silence ....

... followed by more silence ....

Dumbfounded.

I sat with this. I could not pinpoint the answer immediately, but knew I needed to get clarity on this. The answer to this question would be the most impactful part of this book. I got quiet and prayed.

In the earlier section I spoke about the seed of perfection that was planted in my brain and haunted me. The one thing I have learned is that chasing perfection prevents us from truly living. It is all too easy to hide behind the luster of chasing unattainable goals and expectations. When I fell short of meeting a perfectionist goal, it was easy for me to deflect the blame to an external factor. I could link the lack of fulfilling an unreasonable standard to it being someone else's fault. This had me anchored to another series of lies. The more I learned to deflect, the more I never took ownership of this loop of perfection.

From an early age, I struggled with a sense of belonging which led to an identity crisis for me. My father is Creole and my mother is Swiss and German. This is the definition of Creole, according to Wikipedia:

As in many other colonial societies around the world, creole was a term used to mean those who were "native-born", especially native-born Europeans such as the French and Spanish. It also came to be applied to African-descended slaves and Native Americans who were born in Louisiana. (https://en.m.wikipedia.org)

Why did I struggle with this? I did not fit in, and although I wanted to be proud of who I was, I couldn't simply check a box that linked to my heritage. I remember being told I was not "black" but did not look "white." I really struggled with this. I felt like I had to prove I was "black." I remember being infuriated with someone else who was biracial yet more distinct. They did not have to prove their nationality. This internal struggle and identity crisis really impacted me.

As I allow the process of this book to continue to evolve, I can clearly see the impact of my ethnicity and how it impacted my sense of worth. My search for inclusion and belonging is not unique. I spent years trying to "prove" my ethnicity to others. What I have learned is that how I root into who I am is all that matters. I have learned to be unapologetic about who I am. I have learned that I do not have to prove myself to anyone. I have learned that ignorance and fear around ethnicity are not my issues to solve. I have also learned to stand tall and proud in who I am. This has been a long journey for me. We are so lucky to live in a time where inclusion and equality are such strong movements. I grew up in a time where this was not as common as it is today. In school we didn't study strong, smart, and successful women. This movement has changed as well. What I can say is the struggle with worth is woven into gender as well. This is why I am so passionate about changing the narrative around this. Why not root in worth? I literally had no reason not to.

Slowly, the moments that framed this thinking came to mind. Somewhere after the age of seven, I began to feel that I was no longer seen for who I was. I felt pressure to measure up to expectations that were an accumulation of my own expectations as well as those of my parents and other external factors. I was never told I was not as good as my sisters. I was never told I was not enough, yet somehow at an early age I inferred this to be truth. This was when the vicious cycle of being an overachiever began for me.

At the time, I really believed my lack of worthiness resulted from a bad partnership at that big investment firm. I was convinced of it. But as I sat still and listened to the whispers from God, I realized I had been completely wrong about that. What I realized was that the inequity I felt with my former partner was just another way that I reinforced my lack of worthiness in my own mind. I was telling myself that if he really valued me, then clearly he would give me my fair share. So many different excuses could be inserted here, and you might recognize some of them.

"If my partner valued me, then I would feel better."

"If my family showed up for me, then I would feel secure."

Another way to say it is that I had set my energetic vibration very low (i.e. I had lowered my own bar) and I therefore subconsciously connected to a lower vibration.

If you can relate to these statements or recognize that they are similar to ones that you have told yourself, then consider this idea:

When you come up with excuses about why your life isn't going the way you want it to and you blame it on others, you have given away your power. These kinds of statements are basically saying that it is up to the other person to somehow make you feel better. But this is simply not true. We are each capable of so much more, and we are the ones who are responsible for our own lives.

In addition, I hope you can recognize that these statements are really a direct reflection of the lies in your subconscious, and your subconscious mind does not know the difference between a truth and a lie. What I realize now, and what I want to impart to you, is that the most important thing is to recognize your own value within yourself. As soon as you do, you raise your own vibration, and subsequently, begin to attract more of what you want into your life.

The cathartic process of writing this book allowed me to uncover more of the truth behind my block around worthiness. What I can see now is that as we anchor deeper into our calling, our sense of self-worth increases, and it will continue to increase as we evolve in our journeys.

If you are reading this and shaking your head because you can relate to my story, then you are my people. You probably struggle with worthiness as well. I guarantee this book will not appeal to every woman out there, but if my message resonates with you, then I want to remind you that everyone has God-given gifts and talents. Yes, even you! As you step into your worth and become unapologetic about your own value, then you will, undeniably, maximize your financial potential as well.

Are you ready to begin?

Then let's get started.

BUILD YOUR FINANCES

CHAPTER 5

LET'S GET STARTED

My approach to building your finances might seem rudimentary to some, but please stay with me. I have made observations over the years of working in financial services. The one common thread I have noticed is that the mindset you have with money will follow you.

Ask yourself these questions:

What is your current mindset with regard to money?

Does it need an adjustment? And if so, what will you adjust it to?

I spent years looking for the "big break" and the "lucky win," thinking this would be the tipping point for my financial life to thrive. What I discovered is it really comes down to a few distinct habits – discipline, time, and resolve. In the next few chapters I am going to lay out the system I use, one that I assure you that, if followed, will help you shift your relationship with money.

CHAPTER 6

HIRE A FINANCIAL ADVISOR

If you asked me in high school if I knew any financial advisors, the answer would have been followed by a question: what is a financial advisor? My parents did not work with a financial advisor when I was growing up. I stumbled upon this entire industry when I landed the job as the administrative assistant at a big investment firm. I feel so very fortunate for landing that job, as it changed my financial trajectory entirely. I would say most people I encounter do not believe they need a financial advisor or simply think they can do it themselves. Both answers equally sadden my heart. I rarely encounter people who think they do not need a doctor and are capable of administering their own health. Yet I meet people all the time who tell me they do not need a financial advisor. I won't even begin to debunk this from an educational perspective, although that is the obvious rebuttal. I would challenge you to think from an emotional perspective. I rarely encounter clients who have the discipline to handle downturns in the market effectively. Why? Because it involves emotion. It is fascinating to me how people respond when the values of their accounts slide with market movement for money they "do not need anytime soon." What I have learned through experience and studying behavior finance is that most people make the wrong decisions because emotion blinds them from making prudent decisions.

Having a trusted financial advisor can be your voice of reason as well as a person to keep you accountable to your goals. I have encountered so many people who tell me that they do not have the net worth to hire a financial advisor. That may or may not be true depending on your balance sheet, but I would still like to challenge that thinking with you. My advice is to engage with a financial advisor you trust even before you think you are ready. I have several prospects that I work with to offer guidance which enables these women to be clients (for me, ideally, or another financial advisor) someday. It is so important to position your financial balance sheet to progress.

All too often I see people who make decisions on their own and then overspend on their house and cars, which then leads to credit card debt. When you are strapped to a house payment, you limit your options for essential expenses unless you find new income streams (which most people don't). This is just one example of how doing it yourself can lead to choices that might not align with your ultimate goals. I could go on and on with scenarios like this.

Are you equipped to keep up with ever changing tax legislation? Do you really understand if the investment selections you are making are yielding the best tax results for your tax bracket?

Most clients I work with do not even understand their 401k, they simply follow the prompts when they enroll for the 401k. In most cases, people select what option is suggested to them based on the year they want to retire. This may not be the best selection and creates another reason to consult a professional.

The bottom line is this: if you are ready to get your finances in order, then you need to find somebody that you can go to and get help. You don't know what you don't know, so go to the experts. In the long run, this will save you time, pain, frustration *and money!*

The best avenue to find an advisor is by getting referrals from friends and families. This industry is always evolving, but I encourage you to work with somebody who is a little more cutting edge because they might be more adaptable to the many changes that happen with the laws within this industry.

Work to build a relationship with the person you choose. A good advisor will assess where you are on your financial journey by making sure they understand your current assets and liabilities. They will assess your appetite for risk and ascertain how you would respond if the markets drop. They will provide the right allocation given your time horizon and risk tolerance. This trusted advisor will also encourage you to review your assets and liabilities. This review will, ultimately, lead to discussing your goals and creating a strategy to accomplish such goals.

Be prepared to answer questions such as:

Are you looking to buy a home, do you have a home, or do you want to renovate a home?

Do you have children, and are you putting them through school or planning for college?

Do you have any expenses that we should plan for?

What is your goal for saving and amassing wealth?

Are you maxing out your 401k or contributing money into a traditional IRA?

Are you planning for long-term care for you and your loved ones?

Have you created an estate plan for your heirs?

Ultimately, when you hire a financial advisor, you want to be sure to cultivate a relationship with them over time. The better they understand where you are, and recognize where you want to be, the better they will be able to help you.

CHAPTER 7

SET FINANCIAL GOALS

Setting financial goals is very important. If you don't know where you are going, you will never be able to get there. So take the time to create your vision and then write those ideas down on paper.

Write out anything you want to achieve, from the more practical to the completely outlandish. Even if it sounds crazy, shoot for the stars rather than playing it safe. You never know what is possible until you start working toward it, so write down everything that comes to mind.

Once you have written them down, put them into two categories: short-term desires (ones that could be achieved in less than a year) and long-term desires (anything that will take more than a year to achieve). After you've created your list, be sure to share it with your financial advisor so they can help you assess your obligations, determine your flexibility, and work with you to decide the strategy you will use to follow your plan. See Appendix A for worksheets that will help you outline your financial goals.

CHAPTER 8

ASSESS YOUR
SPENDING HABITS

Determining your spending habits is a critical step in the process of financial management. We live in a culture that promotes instant gratification, which makes it very easy to get caught up in the "keeping up with the Joneses" mentality. As you review your expenses, you might be surprised at how much you are spending in different areas.

Here are few real examples from my personal life that were shocking to me:

One day I saw an article in Forbes that stated that Americans waste about one pound of food a day. This really caught my attention. It made me more mindful of my patterns of spending at the grocery store. It actually led me to meal prep and use some of the subscription services that deliver a box containing exactly what you need for the meal.

Another eye opener for me was using premium gasoline when my car didn't need it. Although I was conditioned to believe that the premium was necessary, I realized that it was actually okay to change that habit. As I created my own narrative and new habits, my bank account balances began to reflect the shift.

Once you write your expenses down, you will have a clear picture of everything you're spending. Now is time to prioritize the areas where you want to save. Write out your list based on what you feel is least necessary all the way up to what is most necessary in your life. Then give yourself a 30-day challenge. In 30 days, redirect your spending in one of those areas. For example, give up Starbucks for 30 days, or stop eating out this month. At the end of the month, you will be astonished by how much money you save.

CHAPTER 9

CREATE A BUDGET

Warren Buffett once said, "An idiot with a plan can beat a genius without a plan." With that encouragement, it's time to make a plan, or in other words, to create a budget. If you completed the action step in the previous chapter, you have tracked your spending and now have a much better idea about your patterns and how you handle money. Now, let's get into the basics of creating a budget and what it means to you.

Although the word "budget" may seem like a dirty word to you, I encourage you to reframe how you think and approach budgeting. It may seem like a scary task and feel quite intimidating. If you are like some of my clients, you are probably thinking to yourself that it's going to be hard, and that it will require discipline. If that's the case, then consider this. It will only be difficult until you get into a rhythm with the new process, and if you just follow my methodology, I will help you create a budget that is personal, intentional, and sustainable.

As you begin this process, I want you to give yourself grace, especially if this is something you've never done. It doesn't have to be perfect. There is no right or wrong, and this may take you a while to gain traction. Just remember that any time you do something new, it's like you have sea legs. You feel really wobbly, you're really out of your comfort zone, and you don't think you can do it. Then slowly, you start to gain some momentum and you begin standing a little bit taller with a little bit more conviction. Then you begin to get into a rhythm. Even the best of the best took time to get where they are, so just be patient with yourself.

Second, remember where you are in the calendar. Every month is going to be different, and there are going to be things that you have to plan for based on the time of year. Whatever you need, be sure to build it into your budget. I often have people tell me, "Well, I can't start this because it's my birthday month," or "I can't start this because it's tax season," or "I can't start budgeting because it's vacation and it's summer and I'm on vacation mode," or "I can't start budgeting because it's Christmas time and I've got money that I can't control." You see how easy it is to justify something you don't want to do? There is always something you can use for an excuse. Those excuses are simply lies. The truth is that you can start whenever you want. All you have to do is decide. You work hard for your money. It's time to make your money work hard for you.

Are you ready to begin? Then let's get underway. A budget sheet is included in Appendix B.

Plan to outline a budget for a month.

The first category on your budget is going to be Income. In this category, you will include the income you receive from your paycheck as well as any passive revenue you receive from things such as real estate, investments, or any money you receive from places that are not your primary job. Then find the total of all your income.

It is also important to remember to pay yourself first. The vast majority of the workforce will be offered some sort of retirement savings with employment. Typically, most employers offer a match of your contributions up to certain limits (although every employer is different). No matter what is offered, I encourage you to sign up for the retirement benefits. They will be automatically deducted from your paycheck so you will never miss it. I also encourage you to set a discipline of increasing this percentage every time you receive a wage increase or bonus.

Next you will break down where your money is going on a monthly basis. I like to break it down into these categories: *Essentials, Non-Essentials, Other, and Savings.*

The Essentials column will consist of rent and mortgage, depending on whether you own or lease a home or apartment. In addition, you will need to add the next category, Insurance. This will include home insurance and renter's insurance (if applicable). Still under the Home column will be Electric, Gas, Water and Trash. Then we have Phone, Cable, and Internet. And finally, we have other living expenses, which could include HOA, Lawn Care, or any other expenses related to your home. When you set out your budget for the Home category, be sure to add a little extra money in to be available in case you have any unforeseen expenses. You can also add the subcategories of Health and Dental Insurance, factoring in deductibles and copays.

You can also categorize expenses related to transportation under the umbrella of Essentials as well. The subcategories in Transportation would include Car Payments, Insurance, Gas, Maintenance, Parking, Commuting, Tolls, and so on. And finally, I also suggest that you buffer the amount in the Maintenance category to be prepared for any unforeseen expenses.

The next major category is Non-Essentials. Under Personal, you will include Food, Clothing, Entertainment, and Recreation, Travel, Subscriptions, and Memberships (such as gym or streaming services).

The next category will be Other. This category will include any miscellaneous expenses such as Child Care, Student Loans, etc. Keep this category broad to include anything you haven't accounted for above.

Once you have all of these expense categories listed, be sure to find the total and include that on the form.

Then the last major category is Savings. This will include any Savings Accounts, Emergency Funds, IRA/Retirement, and other. When you subtract your Total Expenses from your Total Income, you may find that you have some extra money. This extra can be placed into these savings categories. The more you save, the more it will compound and grow. So work on saving as much money as you can.

Once you have the initial framework for the budget, you will then create the following categories: Planned, Actual, and Difference. For example, let's say you plan for $500 per month for food but only spend $450. That creates a difference of $50 in that category. Paying attention to your spending habits keeps you accountable to your target goals.

It will also allow you to see where you are underspending, which can then be directed to savings.

Budgets are always a work in progress because you might need to adjust for unforeseen circumstances. But they can also be fun. Here are some helpful hints to make this process more enjoyable for you:

Add a recurring alert to your calendar for the last Saturday of every month. Find the best time on that day (my best time is in the morning), play some calming music, and have a cup of coffee if that makes you feel good. Do all this before you dive into your monthly goals. Keep in mind that the most time-intensive part of the budget process is the first time you do it. After that, you just need to make minor tweaks depending on what has changed from the previous month. You also don't need to import the information over. Simply amend what needs updated.

Make it a family affair by including your spouse or partner. Communication around money is really important and can keep you accountable to your goals. My daughter is a bit too young for this now, but as she gets older, I will include her in the decisions and teach her about this process. If she chooses Disneyland for our trip, for example, that will mean we forfeit another excursion, as I have a budget for such activities.

Sign up for automatic bill pay to pay your bills. It will make that process easier and give you one less task to worry about! It will also help with your FICO score (more on that later).

Challenge yourself to consider whether it is a need or a want when you allocate funds to the Non-Essential category. It helps you to anchor in what is truly important.

Budgets are not about deprivation. They are simply about redirecting money choices toward what you value and what is most important to you. Cutting back on one thing (like Starbucks) gives you extra to use in other ways in your life.

Once you have created your budget, try to stick to it as much as possible for a month. Of course, there may be some adjustments because nothing is set in stone. However, it is a starting point for you to move forward and it can be refined as your situation changes.

Track your Net Worth

The best number to use when tracking financial progress is your net worth. This is calculated by simply subtracting your liabilities from your assets. If your net worth is consistently increasing over time, that's a sign of good financial health. If it is not increasing, go back to your budgeting.

This will give you an opportunity to see what you can adjust to sync up with your long-term goals. Once a year I encourage women to do this exercise as a barometer for how you are doing.

CHAPTER 10

DEAL WITH YOUR CREDIT CARDS

Let's talk credit cards. This topic gets me super excited because this was one of my biggest lessons learned in my relationship with money. If I can help any women avoid this trap, I will feel wildly successful with this endeavor!

This is an area that I'm very passionate about because I fell prey to this. I was young and in college, and there they were – all the tables with the free gifts, and "Sign Up and Pay Later" promises. I was quickly given extended credit that I didn't deserve and definitely didn't need. To make matters worse, I very quickly racked up about $4,000 in credit card debt that I could not manage. At one point, I was even using credit cards to pay my other credit cards. *Big no-no!* I'm not proud to admit it, but I would take out cash advances, which I didn't realize included additional fees. Of course, I also didn't have any idea what the amortization of APR meant. It was a very painful few years for me when I finally hit a breaking point.

Credit is necessary. You need it in order to build your assets such as buying a home or a car. In other words, at some point, you're going to need credit. What I tell people is to be mindful of how you build that credit. Start small. Pay your credit cards off in full, if you can. If you do have credit card debt, one of the best ways to tackle it is to create a plan to start paying it down.

If you have credit card debt, take the credit cards out of your wallet to stop the bleeding. Then become very mindful about reducing the debt. I'm not a big fan of taking those 0% balance transfers. The research shows that it only creates a further loop of debt. The best way to stop debt from building up even further is to stop buying more than you can afford.

Your challenge is to go back to your goal setting and budgeting. Check in with yourself to determine the priority of your funds and your goals. Only spend what you have and don't overextend. As hard as that can be in this age of instant gratification, it is a discipline that you must achieve in order to get out of debt. The ultimate goal is to get to a place where you can pay your credit card debt in full every single month.

About 77% of American households have debt of some kind. Credit card debt in the U.S. has reached $4.03 trillion with an outstanding revolving debt being $1.05 trillion. This is a $197 billion increase from 2013. Credit card debt is revolving debt, meaning that it is an open-ended line of credit as long as you keep your payments current. Revolving debt can be easily abused and accumulated. It allows you to carry a balance month to month and pay minimum amounts to continue the cycle going with the line of credit available. So the catch is that you pay interest on outstanding debt. Typically, a credit card has what is referred to as an APR, which is the annual percentage rate of charge that calculates the interest you pay. It is a finance charge calculated over an annual rate. Several factors come into play when computing this rate which makes it very complicated. What you need to know is that it always works in the lender's favor.

So most people are actually buying things they cannot afford. Now, I hear all the time that people use credit cards to earn points. I get it. We are now living in that day and age, but I challenge you to be brutally honest with yourself. I also want to encourage you to think differently here. If you can pay your credit cards off each month than this strategy is fine. If you carry debt, let's talk about the process to eliminate that debt. You are not earning points if you carry debt. Period.

It has taken me years to get a solid discipline with credit cards as a part of my journey. I challenge you to be very intentional about your use of credit cards.

CHAPTER 11

FICO

Now that we've talked about your goals, your planning, your budgeting, and your credit cards, I want to explain your FICO score. Because I tend to be a little geeky by nature, I am going to get into the nuts and bolts of this topic.

First of all, what is a FICO score?

FICO actually stands for Fair, Isaac and Company, which is a data analytics company focused on credit scoring services based in San Jose, California. It was founded by Bill Fair and Earl Isaac in 1956. Now, it's become the main score that all big banks and lenders use to assess your ability to borrow money and to monitor your track record to determine whether or not you're a good candidate for receiving credit.

Why is this important?

Although your FICO score may not be something that you think about often, it will become very important when you go to buy a car or a new home or any time that you're going to need to apply for a loan. The single most important factor that will determine if you get that loan or not is your FICO score.

Based on your spending patterns and your payment history, you will receive a score ranging from 300-900. Those scores are broken down into five categories:

Poor: 300 to 579

Fair: 580 to 669

Good: 670 to 739.

Very Good: 740 to 799.

Excellent: 800 and above.

It is important for you to find out your score. Although it might be intimidating, I will tell you from personal experience and my personal journey that it is very important to stay on top of this score.

In my case, after that time I racked up credit card debt, my score was between 300 and 579. With a score that low, I wouldn't have been able to get a loan if my life depended on it. That was the time in my life when I had my head in the

76

clouds and didn't want to deal with all the financial issues I was creating. I didn't have a huge amount of debt, but I wasn't managing it well. Although this is a vulnerable admission, I want to share it because I want you to understand that I was exactly where you are. There was actually a time where I got a notice that I needed to attend a course in order to keep my bank accounts from being closed. I call this phase of my journey "Check Jail," or "Check Kiting," and it happened because I wasn't balancing my checking account. As a result, my checks would bounce, and I had to pay a small fortune in fees to the banks. I justified my behavior because I was not intentionally trying to float money. After attending the two-day course, I really felt like a complete loser. I was also in jeopardy of losing the privilege of having a bank account if I did not clean up my act. This caught my attention. I was mostly humiliated. As a result of my careless behavior, I had to use money orders and cash. I would lose my ability to have a checking account if I bounced one more check. I like to think I created the "envelope system" out of that time in my life.

The envelope system became popular when it was shared by Dave Ramsey. A quick synopsis of the envelope system is this: it creates a method of tracking exactly what you are spending in each budget category for the month. You simply add the cash for each budget item for the month in each envelope. At the end of the month, you can see what you have remaining in each category. It also helps to create discipline with money. Most people overspend because they have no one telling them to stop spending. If you allocate $100 for groceries for the month in your budget, then you put that amount in the envelope. At the end of the month, you will know exactly what you have spent.

The good that came out of all of that, though, is that it finally made me stop and think about what I was doing. When I completed that course, I thought to myself, "Okay, I've got to pull it together." I did, and because I figured it out, I know that you can, too. Of course, one of the ways for you to figure it out is to pay close attention to your FICO score.

Let me explain a little more about it, including how it calculated. Your FICO score is based on an algorithm that calculates five components.

1. Your payment record makes up 35% of the score.
2. Current debt balances are 30%.
3. The length of your credit history counts for 15%.
4. New credit cards make up 10%
5. The mix of your credit cards makes up the final 10%

As you can see, your payment record is the largest percentage of the score. That just emphasizes the point that you need to pay your bills on time.

In addition, your debt balance is really important, too, because it affects your credit utilization rate. That percentage is a driving factor for banks to determine whether they will extend credit to you or not. Generally, they are looking for a credit utilization rate below 30%. To put that into real numbers, it would mean that if you have $1,000 of credit available to you, your outstanding debt would be $300 or less.

By now you might be wondering how to find your credit score, so let's discuss that. According to the Federal Trade Commission, you're entitled to one free copy of your credit report every 12 months. There are three main agencies who report the scores: Experian, Equifax, and TransUnion. All you need to do is contact one of those agencies and request a copy of your credit report.

Once you receive the report, it's important to go through it. Sometimes there are inaccuracies, and if there are, you want to dispute them immediately so they can be lifted from your credit report. Credit Karma has a really good guide on how to deal with a dispute on your credit report, and it's free.

Now that you know your score, stop and give yourself some grace. You're doing something that's hard *and likely new*. You're leaning into something that's scary, and you're getting a handle on becoming your own ambassador, so give yourself some credit. You are doing an amazing job and you're learning.

Ready to continue?

Great, let's keep going.

Now that you know the number, think about it like someone who's trying to lose weight. The number on the scale doesn't tell the whole picture, and so it doesn't need to be a beating stick. It's just an indicator. It's telling where you are, and now you have to decide where you want to go. My guess is that most of you want to be in the range of Excellent (800 to 900).

Improving your credit score is like a marathon, not a sprint. It takes time to repair your score, but I promise you it can be done. It took me a few years of hard work and diligence to get my score to be Excellent, and that should give you hope that yours will be the same.

And don't get discouraged if you pay off a debt and don't see a huge change in your score. That happens because credit agencies take time to update. Just keep working on it, a step at a time. It's like building a muscle. It's going to be uncomfortable for a while, but it is worth the pain in the end. Remember, the agencies are looking at your past behavior, so it will take time for your new discipline to sync. Keep at it!

Another metaphor I can use to help you visualize this process better has to do with running. When I was actively running half marathons, I remember people would talk about the way you approach the hill. They said that the way you approach a hill is symbolic of who you are. Some people stop and walk the hill. Some people take it head on. Others will be overly aggressive. Some people just take it one step at a time. Consider that metaphor for where you are in this journey. The way you approach your credit score is like that hill. It's daunting, it's overwhelming, and it seems insurmountable. But guess what? It's not. And I'm going to break down for you some simple ways to improve your credit score.

First, let's debunk a common myth. It is great to be in the fifth category, but it isn't necessary. Many lenders will look at your past history, and as long as you are in the Very Good category, will find it favorable.

Second, let's focus on debt balance. The debt balance is probably going to be the more difficult part to pursue because it will take some time. However, it definitely affects your utilization rate (the amount of credit you're using divided by the amount of credit you have available). Remember that less than 30% is the target. So if you do have credit card debt, you want to get into a consistent pattern of paying it off. It's where planning and budgeting come into play,

The next thing that's important is your payment history. That means paying your bills on time. Fortunately we live in a day and age where we have auto pay. I highly suggest that you take advantage of it and streamline your payments. A good rule of thumb is to set your payment date one day earlier in order to force yourself into a discipline.

One other thing that I want to say about payment history and debt management is to just remember that the past is the past. Although you may have some things to clean up, and you may have some things you want to do differently, instead of using that as a place to get down on yourself or to fall into shame, just allow it to be in the past. Take what you need from it to help cultivate and change the trajectory of where you're going. Keep your eyes focused in a forward direction because that's where you're going. Use your past to create some new habits, make some new decisions, and be more intentional about your money.

Next on the list of improving your credit score: be cautious about anything that might create a hard inquiry on your credit report. I have actually been teased about this, because I'm very, very cautious about doing anything that I know might put an inquiry on my credit report.

For example, recently I was in the market to buy a new vehicle. As I was going to the different dealerships and doing test drives, every salesperson was attempting to profile me, which basically meant they wanted to get my information. Of course, what they were asking for was my Social Security Number. I'm extremely vigilant about not releasing my Social Security Number. Even if you tell them you're just looking, they'll immediately plug it in and run your credit report to see if you qualify for a loan. The problem is that any time you have your credit pulled, it results in a soft inquiry on your credit score. *Soft inquires count too!*

Think about it this way as well. Let's say I went to 10 dealerships, and I gave my Social Security Number to all of them. Although I'm only going to buy or lease one vehicle, I would have had 10 hits on my credit score. Each hit could mean 10 points off my FICO score, meaning I lost 100 points in total when I really would have only applied for credit with one dealership.

This is just an example to show you how important it is to be super vigilant about hard credit inquiries. Always remember that it is your information, it is your score, and you are in control of it. So you can say no.

Let's continue with some information about prioritizing your lending. For example, if you know that you need to move from your apartment and you also need a new car, try not to have both items happen too close together because you're asking for too much credit. That will definitely impact the amount extended to you, and it's also going to impact your score.

Continuing on with some more tips, I will tell you that although you might want to pay down your cards and then close them, that's not the best idea. If you're to a point where you've acquired some self-discipline, and you can keep your spending in control, it actually works in your favor to keep some of those unused credit cards open. The reason why is because those balances aren't being used, so it amps up your credit utilization rate. For example, let's say you have five credit cards, and you use maybe an AmEx, DiscoverCard, or a Visa for most things. However, maybe you have a couple department stores cards like Target, Loft, or Macy's that you don't use as frequently. If you don't close them, that actually works in your favor. Of course, if you have a problem with your spending, then I'd suggest you consider closing them. But most people don't know that leaving those unused credit cards open, as long as there are no fees, can actually impact you positively.

The last thing I'll tell you is be careful of the credit you apply for. It's so easy to get caught up in all these teasers where companies tell you they'll give you two points for every dollar. I have geeked out on that trying to figure it out because the reward system isn't that transparent. The one thing they don't tell you is that after the introduction, they will cap out. If it sounds too good to be true, it probably is. Just be thoughtful and cautious before you sign up.

There is a great resource out there called The Point Guy. He will help you find the card that is best for you based on your spending patterns. The point is that you should always do your research. Don't just open credit cards to open credit cards. A good rule of thumb that I use is to stick to three credit cards. Then you can use one for travel to maximize those benefits, one for personal, and one for business. If you keep it very simple, then it's also easier to transfer the information when tax season rolls around.

CHAPTER 12

LIABILITY MANAGEMENT

One of the suggestions I have is a different approach than other financial advisors or gurus. My suggestion is to work to have enough money to pay your home off at any given point, but I don't believe in paying down your mortgage. Now, obviously, there are some variables such as the interest rate which might impact this decision. However, we've been in a relatively low interest rate environment for a long time, which has meant that you can borrow at cheaper rates.

Start by being mindful of the price of the home that you're buying relative to what you can truly afford. Be brutally honest with yourself about that. It is so easy to get excited and then try and level up to a higher price point when you can't afford it. It happens way too often and it's when people get themselves into trouble. This is the perfect example of why having a financial advisor is so important. You need someone who will be brutally honest with you, a professional who can also run the numbers to help you make a sound decision.

My concept on not paying off your home is I truly believe that you should be able to draw that capital if you ever need it. If something happens and there's a natural disaster, and all of a sudden you're in a position where you need to make a change, if you have all the money in your home, it's going to be much harder for you, and you might be waiting on government agencies for relief. My mindset is that if you have the money to pay your home off, but it's in an investment account or savings account, you can draw from that easier and rebuild or redirect without experiencing hardship. As I mentioned earlier, building multiple income streams is a goal to set your sights on. If you build your investment accounts or saving accounts, you are positioning yourself to potentially earn income (depending on interest rates and investment allocation).

So work hard to put savings away that would allow you to pay off your mortgage if you needed to, and pay your mortgage payments each month on time, but don't pay it off fully. It will give you more flexibility in the long run.

STEP INTO YOUR WORTH

CHAPTER 13

STEP INTO YOUR POWER

We have made it to the third part of the book, which is stepping into your power and amassing your wealth. This is the place where we talk about building your legacy, and it is the part that I'm most excited about. Legacy is greater than currency, in my opinion. In my years in the financial services industry, I've observed interesting layers to the legacy between generations. I have witnessed the generation that earns the money, the generation that maintains the money, and the generation that spends the money. It is my mission to create the generation that amassed its own wealth.

I believe that this dynamic can be changed. We can demystify that whole concept and have wealth continue to grow through the generations. In my opinion, the preservation of wealth is just as important as the creation of wealth. I think that it follows the same theme of budgeting and being intentional, personal, and sustainable about how you do things and how you interface with money. This all begins with being very clear on your short-term and long-term goals.

For many wealthy people, there seems to be a certain point where money loses its luster. Once you can afford whatever you want, it seems that spending it on frivolous desires loses its appeal. *The focus shifts to legacy.* I firmly believe that the way to combat this apathy is to cultivate a sense of legacy and impact into your financial planning process.

Stop and think for a moment about your motive for spending money. What is the long-term impact that you would like to have for your family or even on the world? If you want to make a difference on a large scale, then it starts with learning to live more modestly. People don't amass wealth by spending, they become wealthy and leave legacies when they save. So learning to be frugal and being intentional with your spending is an important habit to develop.

In talking about money and amassing wealth, one of the simple takeaways I want you to have is that you need to be in this for the long haul. The market will go up and down, but over time, your investments can gain consistently. This is true for investments in the stock market or real estate. You just have to stay in the game. If you're looking for a "how to get rich quick" scheme, I don't have those solutions for you. I want to give you solid, sustainable pieces of information to help build your wealth.

My advice is to be very practical and allow growth to occur at a reasonable rate. It's really about time and resolve. If you're trying to create wealth for the long term, the movements in your investment classes, whether it's real estate, the stock market, or art or commodities, will always go up and down. If you have the resolve needed to stomach those cycles, then historically speaking, it's always worked out. I caution you to not get too caught up in the hype. I have seen so many trendy fads that tend to not work out long term. I have seen this with start-up tech companies and cryptocurrency. It certainly can work out for some, but what I have observed is two sides to these risky endeavors. For example, when Bitcoin became mainstream noise, suddenly everyone wanted an allocation to this investment class. Unfortunately, the window of opportunity for this investment happened before it was mainstream news. Those out-of-the-box investments take very qualified, skilled and *accredited* investors. Although they sound exciting, usually you only hear about the wins and not the losses. Don't fall prey to these risky traps, which can mean financial ruin for you. I always like to remind my audience that you have 5 basics ways to invest:

-Currency. This is a money market instrument or cash.

-Loan. This is a bond.

-Business ownership. This would be a stock.

-Commodity. This would be anything that comes from the ground.

-Real Estate. This would exclude your primary residence.

So be cautious with all the schemes out there.

Another piece of advice is that you don't get overly concentrated in any one area. If you have too much focus on one stock, then you will want to consider selling some off to diversify. Although this can be painful when you see the stock prices rise, it is infinitely better than sustaining a huge loss.

Another important consideration as you build your legacy is gaining clarity on what success means to you. It's too easy to fall into the stereotypes of what society may tell us we should be doing or what goals we should strive to attain. I recommend spending some time determining exactly what your measure of success will be and then continue to work toward it.

For me, success is the legacy I intend to leave for my daughter. I want to role model these same principles that I've outlined in the book so that she, too, can be inspired to create a legacy and build her own wealth.

All of these steps require that you have a strong relationship with your financial advisor. When your emotions get the best of you, it's important to have an expert on your side who can give you sage advice.

Lastly, I would like to remind you that even the best of us make mistakes. I recently did not judge the accuracy of disclosure of an investment that I made. I later found out that the business owner who represented the investment opportunity to me was far from honest. It resulted in a painful loss for me. I initially wanted to beat myself up for making a foolish mistake, and I did for a few minutes. After I gained composure, I took note of the areas I could apply as lessons for myself. This will help me in future endeavors. We are all human. I share this with you to disclose I am still a student and I am still learning and evolving with my relationship with money.

CHAPTER 14

SUMMING IT ALL UP

As you have read this book, you have learned about my financial journey, and I hope you have been inspired to begin yours. Financial security shifts your mindset and creates a certain feeling of power. In the beginning, I thought this power was derived from money. Now I realize that money was simply the catalyst. My power came from my mindset shift and *owning my worth*. As long as I allowed my thoughts to stay rooted in the victim mode, nothing changed. It was not until I took 100% ownership of my life that it all changed. All of a sudden, I became my own ambassador. I became CEO of my life and shifted all the beliefs that were not serving me.

Of course, to make that shift, I had to massively change my routine. It began with gaining clarity on my personality type and the fiber of my own being. Then I began to shift my morning routine, which allowed time for me to dream about my future. Thinking vividly and boldly about what my life would look like in five years, ten years, and so on, was empowering. Life has a way of showing up differently when you see it through a different lens. When you let go of what is no longer working or serving you, you can finally begin to become all that you are meant to be.

As I look back on my journey, the accumulation of investing and saving is what began to drive me. I eliminated debt, began growing my retirement and then began growing my savings. I did not necessarily start with an emergency fund like others preach. I just began living as cost efficiently as possible and saving. The savings turned to investing. The investing allowed me to buy my first condo and then my first home. The confidence of each incremental win for me changed the vibration for me. Each time my vibration changed, my efficiencies with work changed too. I began to work a little harder and smarter. The confidence of it began to monumentally build my worth. That self-worth translated in my net worth, and the same thing can happen for you.

I also want to encourage you that "wealth" means different things to all of us. There is financial wealth, social wealth, time wealth, and physical wealth. Most people have the goal to have enough money to last their lifetime. I would say to remember to give yourself grace. Know what wealth is for you and that is what you strive for.

The longest distance in the world is from your head to your heart, and probably the most critical part of all of this is what we tell ourselves and what we believe. We all struggle with our sense of worth, and that uncertainty doesn't change regardless of the stature we achieve in life. However, those insecurities are just a story you are telling yourself, and I'm here to tell you that it is all smoke and mirrors. You are able to rewrite that story at any given time. You are able to step into your power and own your own worth any time you choose to embrace it. Your worth is inherent. It took me years to realize this and even longer to embrace it.

As we come to the end of this book, the one message I hope you take with you is that you are enough.

You are worthy.

You are capable of having the life that you want.

You are capable of being your own financial ambassador.

You are capable of creating wealth that you never thought possible.

Lean into your worthiness. No bag, no shoes, no designer, no belt, no bracelet is going to make worthy. You're worthy simply because you are.

If I can impress that upon you, then this book has been a wild success.

FINANCIAL GOALS

On-going

- ☐ Budget
- ☐ 401ks – any orphaned 401ks
- ☐ Credit card debt
- ☐ Family vacations
- ☐ Home upgrades
- ☐ How much allocating to retirement
- ☐ 529 plans for children
- ☐ Big financial purchases

Retirement

- ☐ Having enough income during retirement
- ☐ Purchasing a retirement property or secondary residence

- ☐ Providing for education of children or grandchildren
- ☐ Determine when and how to withdraw funds from investments to provide for my retirement income

Legacy and Estate Planning Strategies

- ☐ A plan in place for your financial future
- ☐ Ensure my family will be secure in the event of a national disaster
- ☐ Proper amount of life insurance for security for my family
- ☐ Care for family, elder or special needs
- ☐ Estate plan transition
- ☐ Protection for my estate
- ☐ Legacy and financial resources for my family
- ☐ Charitable Contributions
- ☐ Protection for assets from creditors and liabilities

Cash Flow, Liabilities and Investments

- ☐ Plan for debt elimination (all except mortgage)
- ☐ Account Organization
- ☐ Know my cash flow needs
- ☐ Do I have the proper asset allocation for my goals?

- ☐ Maximize tax efficiency for my investments
- ☐ Plan for Capital Gains
- ☐ Plan for business interest of investments
- ☐ Knowing my Net Worth

FINANCIAL CHECKLIST

Jan:

- ○ Set your financial goals for the year
- ○ Set Business/ Career goals for the year
- ○ Set Personal goals for the year
- ○ Set your budget strategy for the year

Feb:

- ○ Review Budget
- ○ Get a copy of your Credit Report
- ○ Get a copy of your FICO Score
- ○ Report any inaccuracies
- ○ Begin a file for your tax documents

March:

- ○ Review your 401k
- ○ Determine if you can increase your contribution
- ○ Try a 30-day challenge to eliminate one "discretionary spending item"

April:

- ○ 30-day challenge results
- ○ Tax Refund or Tax Liability Check in
- ○ Savings plan
- ○ Check in on your financial goals

May

- ○ Review Tax withholding (make any necessary adjustments)
- ○ Save partial rebate/ spend rebate wisely

June

- ○ Learn a new topic pertaining to Finances
- ○ Charitable Giving
- ○ Review Investment Progress

July:

- ○ Check in on goals
- ○ Increase Savings
- ○ Track Net Worth

August:

- Review Employee Benefits
- Review Insurance

September:

- Evaluate your Will and Estate Plans
- Try a new 30-day challenge of one item to eliminate
- Education goals for children

October:

- Goal setting for final quarter of the year
- Allocate money for the holidays

November:

- Beneficiary Review
- Evaluate Health Expenses

December:

- Rebalance Your Portfolio
- Review Net Worth Progress
- Give

BUDGET SHEET

Monthly budget					
Projected Monthly Income			Projected Balance		
Primary Income	$		(income minus expenses)	$	
Extra Income	$				
Total monthly Income	$		Actual Balance		
			(income minus expenses)	$	
Actual Monthly Income			Difference		
Income	$		(actual minus projected)	$	
Extra Income	$				
Total monthly Income	$				

Essential Expenses

Totals	Planned	Actual	Difference
Housing	**Planned**	**Actual**	**Difference**
Mortgage / Rent			
Phone			
Electricity			
Gas			
Water/ Sewer			
Cable/ Internet			
Waste Removal			
Maintenance/ Repairs			
Supplies			
Other			
Subtotal			
Insurance	**Planned**	**Actual**	**Difference**
Home			
Health			
Life			
Other			
Subtotal			

Food	Planned	Actual	Difference
Groceries			
Dining Out			
Other			
Subtotal			

Pets	Planned	Actual	Difference
Food			
Medical			
Grooming			
Toys			
Other			
Subtotal			

Personal Care	Planned	Actual	Difference
Medical			
Hair/Nails			
Clothing			
Dry Cleaning			
Health Club			
Organization dues or fees			
Other			
Subtotal			

Non Essential Expenses

Entertainment	Planned	Actual	Difference
Streaming			
Music			
Movies			
Concerts			
Sporting Events			
Live Theater			
Other			
Subtotal			
Wealth Creation and Savings	Planned	Actual	Difference
Savings or Investments			
Retirement account			
Investment account			
Other			
Subtotal			
Gifts and Donations	Planned	Actual	Difference
Gifts			
Charity 1			
Charity 2			
Charity 3			
Subtotal			

Legal	Planned	Actual	Difference
Attorney			
Alimony			
Payments on lien or judgement			
Other			
Subtotal